001103119

ROGUE
RIVER

Jackson County Library Services
Medford, OR 97501

D0466601

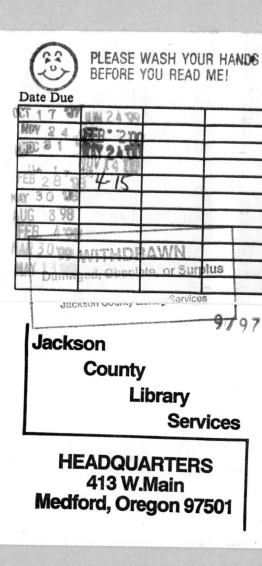

PLEASE WASH YOUR HANDS
BEFORE YOU READ ME!

Date Due

OCT 17	JUN 24 '99		
NOV 24	FEB 2 '00		
DEC 31	MAY 2 '00		
JAN	NOV 14		
FEB 28 '9	4-15		
MAY 30			
AUG 8 '98			
FEB 4 '0			
MAR 30	WITHDRAWN		
MAY 13	Damaged, Obsolete, or Surplus		

Jackson County Library Services

9797

Jackson
  County
    Library
      Services

HEADQUARTERS
413 W. Main
Medford, Oregon 97501

Animals You Never Even Heard Of

PATRICIA CURTIS

SIERRA CLUB BOOKS · SAN FRANCISCO

JACKSON COUNTY
LIBRARY SERVICES
MEDFORD, OR 97501

ACKNOWLEDGMENTS

The author wishes to thank the many knowledgeable people who kindly contributed valuable information to this book: Michael Dee of the Los Angeles Zoo; Tim Sullivan of the Chicago Zoological Society; Peter Shannon of the Olinda Endangered Species Captive Propagation Facility (Hawaii); Helena Fitch-Snyder of the Center for Reproduction of Endangered Species (San Diego Zoo); Bill Konstant of the Philadelphia Zoo; David Shackleton of the University of British Columbia; Jim Doherty of the Bronx Zoo/Wildlife Conservation Park; Michael Davenport of the National Zoo (Washington, D.C.); and Michael Hutchins of the American Zoo and Aquarium Association. The author also offers her sincere thanks to Karen Allen, Kim Hastings, and Pamela Conzo.

And to Paul Loiselle of the Aquarium for Wildlife Conservation (Coney Island, New York), the author extends her deepest gratitude for his unwavering interest, expertise, and assistance.

The Sierra Club, founded in 1892 by John Muir, has devoted itself to the study and protection of the earth's scenic and ecological resources — mountains, wetlands, woodlands, wild shores and rivers, deserts and plains. The publishing program of the Sierra Club offers books to the public as a nonprofit educational service in the hope that they may enlarge the public's understanding of the Club's basic concerns. The point of view expressed in each book, however, does not necessarily represent that of the Club. The Sierra Club has some sixty chapters in the United States and Canada. For information about how you may participate in its programs to preserve wilderness and the quality of life, please address inquiries to Sierra Club, 85 Second Street, San Francisco, CA 94105.

Text copyright © 1997 by Patricia Curtis

Photo credits: © Erwin & Peggy Bauer: 12, 18, 23, 26; © Wolfgang Bayer/Bruce Coleman Inc.: 17; © Tom Brakefield/Bruce Coleman Inc.: 25; © David Cupp: 21, 29, 31; © Gerard Lacz/Peter Arnold, Inc.: 10; © Paul Loiselle: 15; © Hans Reinhard/Bruce Coleman Inc.: 9; © Kevin Schafer & Martha Hill/Peter Arnold, Inc.: 19; © Rod Williams/Bruce Coleman Inc.: 11; © Edwin L. Wright: 13; © Gunter Ziesler/Peter Arnold, Inc.: 27

All rights reserved under International and Pan-American Copyright Conventions. No part of this book may be reproduced in any form or by any electronic or mechanical means, including information storage and retrieval systems, without permission in writing from the publisher.

First Edition

NOTE: Because the animals pictured in this book are extremely rare in the wild, most of the photos were taken in wildlife parks or reserves.

Library of Congress Cataloging-in-Publication Data
Curtis, Patricia, 1923 –
    Animals you never even heard of / Patricia Curtis.
      p. cm.
    Includes index.
    Summary: Presents twelve animals that are rare, threatened, or endangered, including the jabiru, caracal, and babirusa.
    ISBN: 0-87156-594-3
    1. Rare animals — Juvenile literature. 2. Endangered species — Juvenile literature. [1. Rare animals. 2. Endangered species.]
    I. Title.
QL83.C86 1997
591.68 — dc21   96-54480

Book and jacket design: Bonnie Smetts

Printed in Singapore

10 9 8 7 6 5 4 3 2 1

Contents

They Need Our Help Too!

Most of us are familiar with at least some of the world's more famous endangered animals and their struggle for survival. Who doesn't know the plight of the African elephant, or the giant panda, or the humpback whale? And who wouldn't be saddened if the Bengal tiger vanished from the earth forever?

But there are thousands of other, less well known species of animals also struggling to stay alive in today's changing environments. Many of these animals will become extinct (disappear from the earth forever) before we even get to know them. Yet we will feel their loss in some way, because they are all part of the web of life on our planet. In this book, you will meet twelve rare and unusual wild animals that deserve just as much respect and attention as the more famous endangered species.

The main threat that all of these creatures face is the destruction of their habitats — the environments where they find food, water, and shelter and where they mate and reproduce. All over the world, human settlements and activities such as logging and farming are taking over more and more land that used to be wild — land that used to be hunting and

WHO'S COUNTING?

Several organizations monitor the status of animal species. Among them are the World Conservation Union and the parties to the Convention on International Trade in Endangered Species (CITES), including the U.S. Fish and Wildlife Service of the Department of the Interior. Each of these organizations uses its own designations to describe the status of wild species, including those in danger. For example, an animal may be termed <u>threatened</u> on one list and <u>vulnerable</u> on another. See the box on the facing page for definitions of the terms used in this book.

grazing territory for wildlife. In addition, pollution caused by human activity is poisoning food and water sources around the globe. Still another threat that many animals face comes from hunters, who prize them for their meat, skins, or horns.

When an animal's numbers decline, scientists use various designations, such as rare, threatened, or endangered, to describe how close it is to becoming extinct (see the boxes on this page and the facing one).

But the truth is that nobody really knows how many species are being pushed toward extinction. In fact, most of the earth's wildlife has never even been studied. Many animals live in such remote areas that it is very hard to find and observe them. In order to determine the status of a species, researchers must travel to where the animals live, work with local people to count them, learn how quickly they reproduce, observe the condition of their habitat, and estimate the degree of danger they face. This takes many years and costs a great deal of money — and money for such research is hard to come by.

Fortunately, some wild animal species are now protected by laws, such as the Endangered Species Act of the United States, that make it illegal to hunt and kill or capture endangered animals. Also, some international treaties prohibit the export or import of certain animals or their skins or horns. But not all nations agree to abide by these treaties, and not all have enacted their own wildlife protection laws. Even where there are such laws, governments sometimes have a hard time enforcing them, especially if a protected animal lives in a remote area and has always been hunted by local people for food or money.

Many endangered animals are being bred in zoos and reserves to keep them from becoming extinct. Such species survival programs can be successful when they are carefully coordinated by professionals. But, in the end, the best way to save most of the earth's wild animals is to preserve their habitats. Some countries are helping by setting aside special parks and reserves where animals and their environments are left undisturbed. And dedicated individuals and organizations around the world are working to stop the destruction of forests, grasslands, wetlands, and other areas that are home to wildlife.

As citizens of the world, our concern should be for all creatures — the large and the small, the beautiful and the homely, the familiar and the unknown. All are entitled to life, and all need our help. Perhaps if enough people care about them and take the time to work on their behalf, these animals can be saved.

RARE, THREATENED, OR ENDANGERED?

In this book, the following three categories are used to describe how close a species of animal is to extinction:

• **Endangered** means that a species is already in danger of becoming extinct and is unlikely to survive if the present factors causing its decline continue.

• **Threatened** indicates that a species is likely to become endangered if there is no improvement in the current factors causing its decline.

• **Rare** designates a species that exists in such small numbers that it is at risk of moving into the Threatened or Endangered category if the present factors causing its decline continue.

Axolotl

STATUS:

RARE

The greatest threat to the axolotl (<u>Ambystoma mexicanum</u>) is acid rain, which is caused when harmful chemicals in polluted air fall to earth with precipitation. The axolotl's skin, like that of all amphibians, is water-permeable. This means that water — and anything harmful dissolved in that water — is absorbed into the animal's body through the skin.

There's only one place in the world where this salamander can be found living in the wild — Mexico's Lake Xochimilco. The name *axolotl* (ax-oh-LAH-tul) comes from an ancient Aztec word meaning "water monster." Though this "monster" devours only worms and insects, it *is* an odd-looking character, with its mottled black-and-gray coloring and its feathery external gills.

Like its relatives, frogs and toads, the axolotl is an amphibian. Most amphibians go through a change of form, called metamorphosis, as they grow. They begin as eggs and then hatch into larvae, which live in water and have gills, like fish. Eventually, most amphibians develop lungs and turn into air-breathers that can live on land. But the axolotl never gets beyond the larval stage. It grows to be 6 to 12 inches long and even develops legs, but it keeps its gills and remains a water-dweller all its life.

Babirusa

The babirusa (bah-bih-ROO-sah) is about as big as a medium-size farm pig, and wild pigs are its distant cousins, but no other porker has tusks as strange as the male babirusa's. He has two sets: one growing from the top of his snout and the other at the corners of his mouth.

Most babirusas live on the Indonesian island of Sulawesi, where they move about in small family groups near the rivers and swamps of the tropical forests. Their diet consists mainly of tender leaves, insects, and fallen fruit. They forage mostly at night to avoid the local people, who hunt them for food.

STATUS:

THREATENED

On its native island of Sulawesi, deforestation and hunting have brought the babirusa (<u>Babyrousa babyrussa</u>) to near extinction. International treaties now prohibit the export or import of babirusas or their hides or tusks. These treaties, along with breeding programs at some zoos, may help keep this unusual creature from disappearing forever.

10

Caracal

Most cats are good hunters and jumpers. You've probably seen a house cat stalk a bird or leap up easily onto a high wall or fence. But the strong and speedy caracal (CARE-ah-kul) can spring up 6 feet or higher and snatch a low-flying bird right out of the air!

With its tawny coat and its skill at hunting, the caracal lives up to its Swahili name, *simba mangu,* which means "little lion." Long ago, people used to tame caracals and train them as hunting companions.

Smaller than its cousin the Canadian lynx, this fancy-eared wild cat is about 18 inches tall — roughly the size of a fox. The caracal's natural habitat is dry brushland in parts of the Middle East, Africa, and India. There it hunts at dawn or twilight for rabbits, mice, and birds, and sometimes even for larger animals such as deer and antelope, as well as domestic sheep and goats.

STATUS:

RARE

Caracals (<u>Felis caracal</u>) face danger both from trappers, who kill them for their fur, and from farmers, who are taking over their brushland home. Although there are some international treaties prohibiting the export or import of caracals or their pelts, little is being done to preserve their shrinking habitat. Breeding programs in some reserves and zoos are helping to save the species.

Desert Pupfish

STATUS:

ENDANGERED

The already limited habitat of the desert pupfish (<u>Cyprinodon macularius</u>) continues to shrink as desert springs and marshes become polluted and water is diverted to cities and farmlands. But the biggest threat to the pupfish comes from non-native fish that were introduced into their habitat. These fish either eat the pupfish or take their food and nesting places. The good news is that scientists are breeding pupfish in captivity for release into protected reserves.

Millions of years ago, ancestors of the desert pupfish swam in large lakes in what is now the American Southwest. Over time, as the lakes dried up and the land turned to desert, many kinds of fish died out. But the pupfish survived — and today several species still live in the few bodies of water that remain in this harsh landscape.

Desert pupfish have had to adapt to quite extreme conditions. Some live in water as hot as 100°F, while others survive near-freezing temperatures. Pupfish can even tolerate water five times saltier than the ocean.

Pupfish got their name from a scientist who thought these lively little creatures (ranging from 1 to almost 4 inches long) looked as playful as puppies. Although they *are* lively, pupfish are *not* playful when they're defending their territories from intruders!

Golden Lion Tamarin

STATUS:

ENDANGERED

The greatest threat to the golden lion tamarin (Leontopithecus rosalia) is the destruction of its rain forest habitat. To preserve this tamarin as a wild species, many zoos are breeding the animals and sending groups of them to a wildlife reserve in Brazil. There the monkeys are first taught how to live in the wild and then released into a protected area of the rain forest.

A shaggy mane of golden hair gives this creature its name, but its resemblance to the big cat ends there. The golden lion tamarin (TAM-ah-rin) is a sprightly little monkey no bigger than a squirrel. Its call — a musical, birdlike chirp — echoes through the treetops as it leaps gracefully through the canopy of the Brazilian rain forest, gathering fruits, nuts, and insects to eat.

There are many species of tamarins, but in all of them the animals live in close-knit family groups, and the males and females mate for life. Tamarins are unusual in that the father helps take care of the young. Among nearly all other monkeys, the job of child care belongs strictly to the mother. But if you see a tamarin with a baby riding on its back, it's most likely to be the father.

Jabiru

What's a bird to do when it can't sing, call, chirp, squawk, or even quack? Like other members of the stork family, the jabiru (JAB-ih-roo) has no voice at all. Instead, it communicates by clacking its upper and lower bills together. Different clacking beats appear to send different messages, such as greetings or warnings, to other jabirus.

Even though this 5-foot-tall bird can't sing, it *can* dance! At mating time, a male picks out a female and does an elaborate courtship dance, bobbing and twirling and flapping his wings. If she accepts him for a mate, she dances too. Then the male builds a nest in the top of a tree, where the female will lay her eggs.

Jabirus live in the wetlands of southern Mexico, Central America, and parts of South America. They wade in the shallow waters of marshes beside rivers and lakes, searching for fish, frogs, and snakes to eat.

STATUS:

RARE

The jabiru (Jabiru mycteria) is fast losing its habitat as people drain wetlands to build houses, factories, and farms. The best hope for the jabiru is the growing public awareness of the importance of the world's wetlands, which has resulted in new efforts to protect these life-sustaining habitats from development.

18

Komodo Dragon

STATUS:

THREATENED

Because of its great appeal to both scientists and tourists, the Komodo dragon (<u>Varanus komodoensis</u>) is protected by the Indonesian government. Still, this creature has such a limited range that it could easily be wiped out by a natural disaster or by a large influx of human settlers, who would destroy its habitat or compete with it by killing its natural prey.

With its scaly body and long, forked tongue, this fearsome creature looks like a prehistoric monster that just stepped off a movie screen. In fact, its ancestors walked the earth with the dinosaurs, and the Komodo (ko-MO-doe) dragon has hardly changed since then. The world's largest lizard, it measures up to 10 feet long and weighs as much as 300 pounds.

This remarkable animal was unknown to most of the world until early in this century, when fishermen reported seeing giant "dragons" on the tiny Indonesian island of Komodo. This is one of the six hot, dry, rocky islands where these huge lizards live.

Komodo dragons eat mostly carrion (the bodies of animals that they find already dead), but they also catch live prey, including goats, deer, birds, crabs, and snakes. Despite their great size, Komodo dragons are fast, and they're powerful enough to take down a water buffalo — and sometimes even an unlucky human!

Markhor

STATUS:

ENDANGERED

Markhor (<u>Capra falconeri</u>
<u>heptneri</u>) are hunted not only
for their meat but for their
horns, which are considered
great trophies. Another
problem they face is that, as
human settlements spread into
their territory, they must
compete for food with domestic
animals. Efforts are now being
made to protect the species
through laws and international
agreements.

With its magnificent corkscrew horns and shaggy beard, the male markhor (MAR-kore) looks every inch a stern old mountain king. And he doesn't hesitate to use those heavy horns against other males in battles over females.

Largest of all the wild goats, the markhor stands almost 4 feet tall at the shoulder and can weigh more than 200 pounds. Despite its size, it travels nimbly across the steep, rocky slopes of its mountain habitat: the high forests and alpine meadows of Kashmir, Afghanistan, and other countries of southwestern Asia.

The markhor's hair is short in summer and long and silky in winter. Adult males have long beards and heavy manes.

In the Persian language, the word *markhor* means "snake eater." But why the animal was given this name is a mystery — no markhor has ever been known to eat a snake! Like other goats, the markhor nibbles on grass, herbs, and shrubs.

Okapi

STATUS:

RARE

Because much of its rain forest home is being taken over for farming or destroyed by logging, the future of the okapi (Okapia johnstoni) in the wild is uncertain. The good news is that some okapis have found a safe haven in the newly created Okapi National Park in Zaire, and several zoos have undertaken breeding programs to help save this species.

The okapi (oh-KAH-pee) looks as if it's trying to be two different animals at once. It has a long neck and big ears like its relative the giraffe, yet it's about the size of a zebra and has zebra-like stripes on its forelegs and rump.

While giraffes and zebras live on the African grasslands, the okapi makes its home in the rain forests of Central Africa. It was named by the pygmy people of the area, who were the only ones to know of the animal's existence for hundreds, perhaps thousands, of years.

The shy, quiet okapi moves about the rain forest only at night, browsing on a wide variety of leaves, bark, and fruit. With its dark color and stripes, it blends easily into the shadows, where it can hide from its enemies: leopards and humans.

Pudu

Some people think the pudu (POO-doo) looks a bit like a dog. It *is* about the size of a small terrier and *does* have thick fur and short, sturdy legs. But, in fact, the pudu is the world's smallest deer. This gentle creature stands just over a foot tall and weighs only about 20 pounds. Unlike most deer, the male pudu doesn't grow a full set of antlers; instead, he grows two small spikes on his head.

Pudus live in pairs or small family groups in the dense temperate forests at the foot of the Andes Mountains, along the west coast of South America. They spend the daylight hours in the safety of the forest undergrowth, venturing out into more open spaces only at dusk or nightfall to browse on leaves and twigs.

STATUS:

THREATENED

International treaties prohibit the export or import of the pudu (**Pudu pudu**), but other threats to its survival remain. Hunted by people for its hide and meat, the pudu is also preyed upon by pumas, foxes, and domestic dogs. Perhaps most important, the pudu has lost 90 percent of its forest home to logging. Fortunately, some pudus now live on reserves, and they are being bred in captivity.

Pygmy Loris

In the Pacific region known as Indochina, and on the nearby islands of Indonesia, live some shy little animals with hands like monkeys and big, soulful eyes. Early Dutch settlers in Indonesia were so amused by the animals' faces that they named them *loeris*, which means clown.

The smallest species, the pygmy loris (PIG-me LOR-iss), makes its home in the rain forests of Vietnam and Laos. It is active at night, when it ranges through the trees, feeding on leaves, insects, and lizards. Very little is known about this creature because it lives in remote regions where few researchers have been able to go and study it.

All lorises belong to a group of rare animals called prosimians, which have lived on the earth for millions of years. You might say that prosimians are our living ancestors, since all other primates — monkeys, apes, and humans — are descended from them.

STATUS:

THREATENED

During the Vietnam War, many pygmy lorises (<u>Nycticebus pygmaeus</u>) were left without food and nesting places when much of their jungle home was destroyed by defoliation — the spraying of chemicals by the military to strip trees and other plants of leaves in order to expose enemy locations. Today, Vietnam has given some legal protection to the pygmy loris, and a movement to restore and preserve the forests has begun.

Red Uakari

STATUS:

ENDANGERED

Like many other species, the red uakari (Cacajao rubicundus) is losing its rain forest home to logging and human settlements. It is also in danger from the local people, who hunt this monkey for food. Recent scientific research on uakaris may inspire more interest in saving them. And conservation programs under way in Peru and Brazil may help preserve what is left of their shrinking habitat.

This gentle monkey's face and bald head are naturally red to begin with. But when the animal gets excited or frightened, they turn even redder!

Native to the rain forests of Peru and Brazil, the red uakari (wah-KAH-ree) is a slender little monkey less than 2 feet tall, with long, brown hair and, unlike other New World monkeys, a short tail. It spends most of its time in the forest canopy — the tops of the trees — where it runs along the branches on all fours. Its diet consists mainly of fruits, nuts, and leaves.

The red uakari is one of only a few species of uakaris, all of which are very rare. Uakaris live together in extended family groups called troops, which may consist of from 10 to 30 or more members.

Index